A NOTE TO PARENTS

Reading Aloud with Your Child

Research shows that reading books aloud is the single most valuable support parents can provide in helping children learn to read.

- Be a ham! The more enthusiasm you display, the more your child will enjoy the book.
- Run your finger underneath the words as you read to signal that the print carries the story.
- Leave time for examining the illustrations more closely; encourage your child to find things in the pictures.
- Invite your youngster to join in whenever there's a repeated phrase in the text.
- Link up events in the book with similar events in your child's life.
- If your child asks a question, stop and answer it. The book can be a means to learning more about your child's thoughts.

Listening to Your Child Read Aloud

The support of your attention and praise is absolutely crucial to your child's continuing efforts to learn to read.

- If your child is learning to read and asks for a word, give it immediately so that the meaning of the story is not interrupted. DO NOT ask your child to sound out the word.
- On the other hand, if your child initiates the act of sounding out, don't intervene.
- If your child is reading along and makes what is called a miscue, listen for the sense of the miscue. If the word "road" is substituted for the word "street," for instance, no meaning is lost. Don't stop the reading for a correction.
- If the miscue makes no sense (for example, "horse" for "house"), ask your child to reread the sentence because you're not sure you understand what's just been read.
- Above all else, enjoy your child's growing command of print and make sure you give lots of praise. *You are your child's first teacher — and the most important one. Praise from you is critical for further risk-taking and learning.*

— Priscilla Lynch
Ph.D., New York University
Educational Consultant

For Martha and her apple tree
—J. Marzollo

For Dale, my friend and birthday mate
—J. Moffatt

Library of Congress Cataloging-in-Publication Data

Marzollo, Jean.
    I am an apple / by Jean Marzollo ; illustrated by Judith Moffatt.
        p.   cm.—(Hello reader! Level 1)
    "Cartwheel Books."
    Summary: Depicts a bud on an apple tree as it grows into an apple, ripens, is harvested, and provides seeds as a promise for the future.
    ISBN 0-590-37223-8
    1. Apples—Juvenile literature. 2. Apples—Life cycles—Juvenile literature. [1. Apples.] I. Moffatt, Judith, ill. II. Title.
III. Series.
SB363.M35   1997
634'.11—dc20   97-6010
                                                                                              CIP
                                                                                              AC

10 9 8 7 6 5 4 3 2 1
Printed in the U.S.A.   24
First printing, September 1997

I Am an Apple

by Jean Marzollo
Illustrated by Judith Moffatt

Hello Science Reader! — Level 1

SCHOLASTIC INC.

Cartwheel
·B·O·O·K·S·®

New York   Toronto   London   Auckland   Sydney

I am a red bud.
I live on a branch
in an apple tree.

I grow in the rain.

I grow in the sun.

unfold.

'm an apple blossom!

I have five petals.
I am beautiful.

In time,

my petals

fall to the

ground.

Now I am a small apple.
I hang by a stem.
The stem brings me water
and food.

I grow
bigger

and
bigger.

My tree is full
of apples.

Once we were green.
Now we are red.
Red, redder, reddest.

Most apples
are picked
by farm workers.
Truckers drive
us to market.

Apples come in different shapes and colors.

Some are sweet.
Some are sour.

Applesauce is made
from apples.
What else is made
from apples?

Each apple has a
star of seeds inside.
The star has five parts,
just like the flower.

If you plant apple seeds,
what do you get?

Apple trees!

I am an apple.

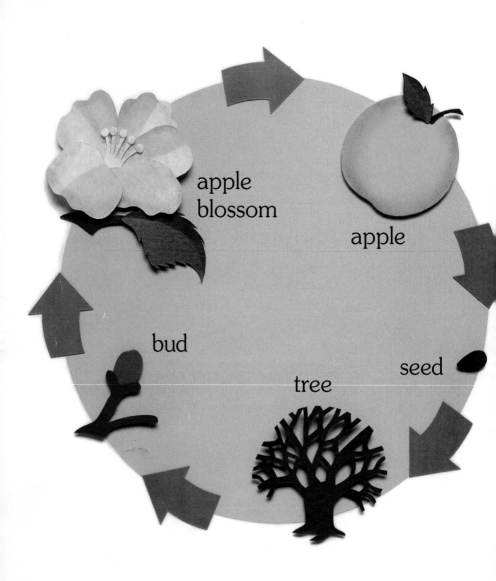

apple
blossom

apple

bud

seed

tree

Can you tell a story about me?